Lunch in Chinatown

Mary Bonina

Červená Barva Press
Somerville, Massachusetts

Copyright © 2024 by Mary Bonina

All rights reserved. Poems in this chapbook can be reprinted only by permission from the author, and may not be reproduced for publication in book, magazine, or electronic media of any kind, except in quotations for the purpose of literary reviews or articles.

Červená Barva Press
P.O. Box 440357
W. Somerville, MA 02144

editor@cervenabarvapress.com
http://www.cervenabarvapress.com

Visit the bookstore at:
http://www.thelostbookshelf.com

Cover photo: Abbi Sauro

Production: Allison O'Keefe

ISBN: 978-1-950063-88-8

Also by Mary Bonina

Living Proof: Poems
Clear Eye Tea: Poems
My Father's Eyes: A Memoir

To my sons, Gianni Bonina-Pawlak and Andrai Pawlak Whitted, who embrace diversity enthusiastically in their lives and work.

CONTENTS

Introduction by Patrick Sylvain	IX
Preface: Where the Poems Come From	XI
Quotation: Lisel Mueller	XII
Lunch in Chinatown	3
37 Bennet Street	4
Examples	5
Composition	6
Teaching the Past Tense	8
A Couple: More of the Past	9
English Lesson Plan: Present Perfect	11
A Favorite Question	13
Spring Words	15
Fashion Sense	17
Practicum	19
Savant at Whole Foods	22
Drift	24
Acknowledgments	25
About the Author	27

INTRODUCTION

In Mary Bonina's chapbook, the title poem, "Lunch in Chinatown," captures a moment of bonding and understanding between two individuals against the backdrop of a cold winter day in Boston's Chinatown. The poem begins with a vivid depiction of the day after Christmas, where the sidewalks are described as "slippery with snow and ice." This setting establishes a cold and challenging environment, reflecting the external conditions that the characters, Wei Wei in particular (as well as the other adult students), must navigate. Bonina's chapbook is a gem, a lesson in thoughtfulness, revealing the subtle encounters of an immigrant who is presented as a person instead of a case study. They shared laughter at "what they have in common, " despite the language barrier, highlighting the universal nature of human connection. *Lunch in Chinatown* is a poignant exploration of valued human connections, understanding, and shared humanity in the face of cultural and linguistic differences. Bonina becomes the astute poet who is at once a keen custodian as well as a non-intrusive linguistic ethnographer, opening her professional and yet intimate world through the precise power of poetry.

In "Teaching the Past Tense," Bonina delves into the poignant narratives of individuals from Haiti, Guatemala, Ethiopia, and China, reflecting on their unique journeys and the weight of their pasts. The struggle to convey abstract concepts like philosophy or navigate cultural differences is artfully captured in "Examples," highlighting the challenges of communication and understanding. The poem "English Lesson Plan: Present Perfect" uses humor to illustrate the nuances of language learning. Bonina guides the class through a lesson on the present perfect tense using a cartoon about the Lintner family. The blurring of reality and hallucination in Margarita's story adds depth to the exploration of language and its impact on perception.

Lunch in Chinatown invites readers to savor the beauty in the commonplace, finding poetry in the aisles of a supermarket and the heart of a community. The poet's eloquent verses breathe life into the seemingly mundane, turning lunchtime into an exploration of the extraordinary moments hidden within our daily routines. Since the chapbook is only a "lunch," I would like to warn readers who would want to have a poetic dinner with the author.

Patrick Sylvain
Assistant Professor, Global/Transnational
Postcolonial Literature
Simmons University
Lead Author, *Education Across Borders*, Essays
Beacon Press, 2022

WHERE THE POEMS COME FROM....

One of the many jobs I've held while trying to balance a writing life with financial and other needs has been that of freelance English as a Second Language teacher to recent immigrants working in Boston hospitals and banks, and as Creator/Director of the Cambridge Public Library Literacy Project. My students were adults new to the United States, and they came from China, Haiti, Central America, Africa, Sicily, Poland, and elsewhere, students who spoke some sixteen different languages and held a variety of positions including, clerk, cashier, cafeteria worker, phlebotomist, medical researcher, custodian, patient transporter, parking attendant, and nurse's aide. Many of those I taught had held professional positions in the countries they'd left—some were engineers, doctors, and teachers; coming to the United States, not knowing the language, most of them had no choice other than to take service jobs to support themselves and their families.

Most—although not all—of the poems in this collection involve the students who were in my Chinatown classes at the medical center, where they worked. Some were inspired by my commute on the subway, or by walks through neighborhoods where residents who'd immigrated from many countries lived, worked, or shopped.

I loved teaching these students and had great empathy for their situation. Many had fled poverty, political troubles, and even famine that plagued their homelands. I suppose I was motivated to help them partly by my own family's experience, ancestors who immigrated from Sicily and Ireland, who had to negotiate a new culture and new language themselves. So, I took my role seriously, always prepared with a lesson plan that I had labored over.

Often though, after just a few exchanges of dialogue, I would have to abandon my outline. Desperate to learn the language, to be able to navigate in a new culture, my students would interrupt me with their own pressing needs for specific vocabulary or grammatical construction; when they did follow my lead, they asked questions and offered interpretations and possibilities I had not anticipated when planning my classes. I realized that this was a survival skills course, and eventually I accepted that and gained more confidence and got comfortable with what I had initially seen as interruptions.

I began then to find it exhilarating, letting my teaching benefit from an improvisational style. I began to feel like a jazz sax player must, taking my cues from my students and creating something new, building upon what they offered me. I felt, too, like I was writing a poem, recognizing that familiar process of one word, one thought, leading to another—often unanticipated—recognizing endless possibilities and finally settling on specific ones, in a moment of revelation. I learned how to encourage the flow, to go with the stream of consciousness, and how to bring it back to my intended lesson. For example, the poem "English Lesson Plan: Present Perfect" is, as the title suggests, about teaching the present perfect tense, a task that has stymied many an English teacher, even those working with native speakers of the language. That poem and the poem "Spring Words" just might be the best examples in the collection that illustrate the way I would allow a riff to take its natural course, yet bring it back eventually to the original theme.

The collection of poems is titled *Lunch in Chinatown* after the fact that one of my teaching sites was on the edge of Chinatown, and students there often attended my classes during lunch break, "brown-bagging it." I hope you will learn from them, as I did.

Mary Bonina
May 2024
Cambridge, Massachusetts

Note: This essay was published in a slightly different form on Ellen Steinbaum's blog. (blog.ellensteinbaum.com) in a feature titled "Reading and Writing and the Ocassional Recipe."

"Because the story of our life
becomes our life

Because each of us tells
the same story
but tells it differently

and none of us tells it
the same way twice."

                Lisel Mueller

Lunch in Chinatown

Lunch in Chinatown

The day after Christmas, the sidewalks
were slippery with snow and ice.
Wei Wei took my arm as we started across
Kneeland Street to Tyler for Dim Sum.
At first I didn't know why she would hold on,
not until I looked down, making sure
my feet were on safe ground and I saw
she wore bright yellow summer shoes,
like ballet flats, but with hard soles.

The air was bitter cold,
smoky and scented with ginger and sesame,
and ginger and sesame flavored noodles
were what we ordered, both of us pointing
to the same thing on the menu, the *Number 12*
translated into English for me.
And we laughed at what we had in common—
certainly language wasn't it.
I knew nothing about Wei Wei then,
not even that she had worked as a doctor
in China's largest hospital. I only knew
she didn't like the cold,
that she was afraid of falling,
and that she wanted to learn English very much.

No. 37 Bennett Street

A quiet moment on the third floor
in the stuffy makeshift classroom on the edge of Chinatown
and something in one of the shopping bags in the corner
moves.
    There are always shopping bags:
    the students work at the medical center,
    buy groceries in the Chinese markets at lunch hour,
    save time/money.

Winston stands up. It's his bag.
"Don't worry. It's my fish."
Then he's holding up a plastic zip-lock bag
full of water and angel fish, saying,
"I mind fish," meaning
it is his hobby.

Examples

Pressed to explain the word *philosophy*
on page thirty-eight in the English practice book,
Andre, a Haitian, helps me out.
"Descartes?" he asks. He knows,
can explain to the others who speak French.
Then all I have left to do is
find a way to help the Chinese understand.
First I try Lao Tsu, then I try Confucius.
Yes, Confucius! Confucius works for them all.

                2.

On another day I ask:
"Have you ever met a famous person?"
Felix from Guatemala says he once met B.B. King.
Ethiopian Hagos says he met the Governor.
And Andre says, "I met Superfly Snuka."
              "Superfly Snuka?"
"A wrestler," Andre says, explaining.
"I saw him on Kneeland Street buying a lottery ticket
the day before his match at Boston Garden.
He shook my hand."

Composition

Ana's first job in the U.S.,
she took care of old women
sick with pneumonia
on a back ward at City Hospital.

For meals they got broth
that had the look and aroma of nothing.
Her job was to make them swallow it.
Then she marked the chart, called it eating.

If they were able she could take them
down the long corridor to the solarium.
She knew how not to look
into the rooms as they passed by.

She tried not to hear them moaning
and calling to her—the others—
the ones she was not supposed to feed.

She didn't get better assignments,
delivering *Get Well* cards and letters,
Lindor chocolate assortments, or roses and fern
in milk glass vases, and those dish gardens,
the ones that went home with those who recovered,
succulents that would live forever.

She was just married then.
She kept her wedding ring in the pocket of her coat
in a locker down in the basement near the morgue.
The rule was *No Jewelry*, if you worked on a ward.

She noticed sometimes, when she lifted
the spoon to a dying woman's lips,
without that ring on her finger
her hand felt too light, made her think
that she wasn't in the world anymore.

Teaching the Past Tense

Let's talk only about the past today:
"Where *were* you born?"

They begin talking all at once, saying
the names of the countries they came from:

Haiti. Guatemala. Ethiopia. China.

Ana puts her right hand to her forehead, trying
to keep her eyebrows from knitting together,
remembering how she found her way out,
left Central America, came to Boston,
after she lived for a time in New Orleans.

And Andre shudders, unable to forget
Haiti, the Duvaliers, the earthquake.

The Chinese women in class
used to have traditional names.
Here, they were given American names,
Nancy, Jenny, and *Karline*, who says an Irish man,
someone her father knew, named her.

Hagos, the Ethiopian says—not somberly,
just matter-of-factly— "My country.
Lot of people dead."

A Couple: More of the Past

How did you meet your wife? I ask Andre, the younger of the two Haitian men in class. Past tense was the lesson today. The history of love and marriage seemed as good a subject as any for practice. I had called on Andre because I was certain he had a wife. I didn't know yet about the others, but Andre's wife, Giselle, was in my *Beginner's* class, still learning the present tense of the verb "to be."

"How did I meet my wife? My wife, I see her on the street."
"You see her?" I ask.

He struggles, then corrects himself, begins to speak more carefully.

"I saw her," he says. "Then…"
He hesitates, shrugs, just as he always does, whenever he knows he is going to make a mistake.

"She likes to go to the movies. So, afternoons—two o'clock—we go to the movies."

Late in the day the sun streams in on this wing of the building where class is held for hospital employees.

"Past tense. Past tense," I coach. I know they have no time or money to go the movies now.

Although it is my rule to correct my students, I enjoy Andre telling his story, just as if he were now, at this time in his life, meeting his wife, as if telling me, one of his friends, what is new with him.
He puts me on that bright street brimming with activity in Port au

Prince. I can see Giselle, a young girl with her friends all standing around her. They don't giggle. They feign aloofness.
And Andre approaches the group, as he approaches his English class: shyly and respectfully.

Everyone in the makeshift classroom smiles.
Who knows what this room is generally used for?
Occupational therapy? A place for seminars?
Family conferences? This moment though,
the room is reserved for Andre's story.

English Lesson Plan: Present Perfect

1.

The Roz Chast cartoon in The New Yorker
shows a goofy mother, father, children
seated all in a line, pressed tight together
between sofa arms, staring at the TV.
"The Lintners," the caption says,
"Stuck on the sofa since 1987."

I show it to the class, thinking, will they laugh?
The clipping is an example I use
to illustrate the present perfect tense.
It gets passed around. Everyone nods,
very, very serious about learning
the present perfect tense.

Q. "How long have The Lintners been stuck on the sofa?"
A. "The Lintners have been stuck on the sofa since 1987."

2.

Stuck on a sofa, *hypnotized* by TV brings up new
vocabulary. I explain *to be in a trance*.
This leads to *sleepwalking*, then to *daydreaming*,
and finally to *hallucination*.

Hallucination inspires Margarita to tell a story:
her last job—the State Hospital—there was a man
who had lost his mind when he lost his wife.

Whenever he got angry, says Margarita,
he would think that he was still in Cuba,
still in the hot sun. He would mime
cutting sugar cane with his machete.

3.

Someone is using the word *cuckoo*.
I must explain that it is the name of a bird,
and not the right word to describe someone who is ill.
The Haitians think I'm talking about the owl, a bird that
frightens them, its face, the face of a cat, the eyes...
When they say, *nocturne*, I know
their mistake, draw an owl on the chalkboard.

4.

And the lesson for the day ends this way,
me saying, "It is an owl, not a cuckoo.
Haven't you ever seen a clock shaped like a house
and a little bird comes out of the upstairs window singing,
Cuckoo, Cuckoo! the exact number of times
to tell the hour? The present perfect tense, like time
goes on and on, or like The Lintners, or the man who has
been cutting sugar cane ever since his wife died, or
the owl that has been awake all night long, hooting."

A Favorite Question

One day in class Mei Xing asked me
about her Boston address. She struggled,
her brow wrinkled, and she told me
she lives on St. Botolph St.
She wanted to know, "Why?" So, I
asked, "Don't you like where you live?"

I missed the point, so she did what I do
when I'm not being understood, got up
from her seat, went to the easel,
made a diagram, used a lot of drama,
and underlined the abbreviations for
Saint and *Street*, asking again, "Why?"

She wanted me to know that
I had missed the obvious.
It was the plain and simple fact that
saint and *street* share the same abbreviation.
I must say, I had never considered that,
but clearly Mei Xing was shocked.

"A saint is like the Buddha, yes?"

I knew nothing about the saint, but
Mei Xing was arguing Botolph's case, upset
about reverence denied, which must be
deserved, for him to have been given such a title.
It upset her greatly to bring a saint down
to street level. And then I remembered

reading of the thousands of the faithful,
who flock every week to Chiang Mai Temple,
bearing gifts for The Buddha, prostrating
themselves before the statue's feet,
offering money, jasmine garlands, praying,
and making their petitions known.

Spring Words

I'm in trouble right away,
talking about flowers,
starting with *lily of the valley*.
But in spring, don't
we risk beginnings?

Remembering French lessons
and a once popular perfume,
I say to the Haitians:
Muguet des Bois, and they
smile, sweet as the flower's scent.

Where is the valley?
Was there a real place
where it was baptized?

What about this little lily,
the blossom's shape, the way
it grows? A trumpet demanding
a part in the ensemble.

In describing the bloom I'm afraid
now that I've mentioned *trumpet*,
I can't leave out the rest of the band.
It becomes necessary to introduce
jazz, *parade*, and *concert*, too.

When I try *cluster* for the way
the flowers grow, I must think
of *stars, constellations* lighting up
a clear night sky. And I must
mention the neighbor's front yard,
where *dandelions* and *bluebells* seed
themselves all over the manicured lawn.

Someone always gets a discussion moving
on a different track, a related subject,
one that comes with its own set of problems.

I face then the vocabulary of what flowers
will do to a person, and not just someone
in love. I've got to contend with *allergies*
and *antihistamines*, a barrage of symptoms
thrown at me—the *tearing* and the *sneezing*—
the miserable way some people feel in spring
even if they are in love.

Fashion Sense

The students in this class all women
and only the one from Poland might be
called stylish. She paints her fingernails
a color she says is called
I'm Not Really A Waitress.

At Christmas she buys the teacher a gift,
a wool challis scarf, and another day
remarks, seeing me enter the classroom,
You look good wearing black.

But even she is sensible, once
bringing to class a loaf of Polish Rye,
the lesson, something to do with bread.

Next to her, an elegant Haitian woman
keeps trying to hold onto a word.
A natural beauty, yet her manner is not.
She admits to everyone, she loves the movies.

Examine, too, her grace and her French
accent, nearly Parisienne. And do not
ignore the obvious, that even
a white uniform looks good on her.

Who would be surprised to know
that now, learning English,
my Chinese students want words
to describe bolts of cloth they remember

nudging past a needle at the sewing bench,
stitching a collar, a hem, an ornamentation.

Without my help they know English
words like wool, cotton, rayon and linen.
Interested in fabric, style, craft,
these tailors, dress and lace makers,
weavers and knitters,
have embroidered flowers on silk.

What they want from this lesson is
something more subtle, asking me
how to say *spots, lines, squares*.
I give them new words then:
stripe, plaid, polka dot, and
the more delicate, *dotted Swiss*.

I cut up old clothes and bring to class
swatches to show them *herringbone,
hound's-tooth, black watch*, and *glen plaid*.

They admire my hair, curling on a humid day,
but I love theirs, straight and silky in any weather.

Practicum

The train stops at Porter.
A group of children, a field trip
from a day care center, board and
immediately start counting aloud
for their teacher—"one, two, three, four..."
the number of station stops on the subway map.

This is ordinary, yet I can't help smiling
or noticing the man next to me, smiling, too.
I think: he has not lived in the city long,
is too open, looking right into my eyes.
He is not afraid of asking either:
"How do you call that—what they are doing?"

"Numbers," I say. "Do you speak Spanish?"
"*Numero*? Isn't that it?"

"No. Portuguese. We say, *contas*, what they do."

"Oh! Counting. They are counting," I say.
"Or, you can say, *they count*."

The man feels sure he may ask now for other words,
words more pressing for him at the moment.

"Also, for example," he begins,
"I go to meet you and you are not there.
How can I say this?"

So, it is about a missed connection,
someone's disappointment—his own—
or his excuse for being someone else's
that he wants to talk, to know proper form,
the right words, to smooth things over.

Always, I would rather imagine than ask
for context, so I invent that a woman is involved.
I don't wonder if he stood her up on purpose—
not that—he is too concerned with
getting it all just right.

You can believe what you want:
that he missed an appointment
with his doctor, lawyer, or someone
he'd hoped to work for. I prefer to believe
he owns no watch rather than that
he was afraid of some meeting.

The children keep on practicing numbers,
finding everything in the world can be counted:
how many tunnel lights flash past their window,
noticing several passengers are wearing hats,
that some do not have a seat, revising
all the time, for our world is in flux. And when
the train emerges from underground, and onto
Longfellow Bridge, they begin then,
a census of sailboats on The Charles.

The Portuguese man is leaving.
"Goodbye. Nice speaking with you," he says,
silent after, yet his lips keep moving,
just as if he is praying, only I think instead
he is going over the words I gave him, practicing,
repeating in his mind so he won't forget,
saying, *When I got there you were gone.*

Savant at Whole Foods

At the supermarket Express
checkout, my two items on the counter:

a carton of milk, some tomatillos—
on the tomatillos, no label.

The cashier needs a code to calculate cost.
I say, "tomatillos." She shakes her head,

calls out to a clerk passing by,
holds up the eco-plastic bag of fruit.

She asks for the code. "What number?"
The man recites the number. He says,

just as I have, "tomatillos." Then the price
appears on the cashier's screen.

I want to know if the man knows
the code for every item sold in store.

And he says he does. "Really."
And because I'm impressed,

he wants me to know how much
more he knows. For instance, coffee.

The store sells twelve kinds, fresh ground.
He can identify each one by its aroma.

A whiff of Harar from the Ethiopian highlands
is not the same as Arabian Mocha, grown

in the mountains of Yemen. He distinguishes
Indonesian varieties—Sumatra, Java, Sulawesi,

catches the scent of Guatemalan Antigua Volcanic
and from Costa Rica, Margarita and Cashier.

The man know also, this fruit I'm buying
these small green globes have existed before

humans ever did, fossils found fifty million years
before, and he knows the Aztecs named the fruit.

Drift

Tonight the streets are dead.
I give the world the cold shoulder,
the frozen stare. There is clean snow on my brow.

At LA BOTANICA AND MARKET I feel warmer
seeing crates of limes and lemons at the door.
There's a family at work inside:
blood of a hot country travels in their veins.
On shelves there are Chile pepper condiments.

My nose pressed against the glass
I watch a young boy juggling
Florida "Sunkist." I begin to thaw.
When he sees me, his timing is destroyed
and he drops them, hugs himself to show me
he is sorry I'm out in the storm.

ACKNOWLEDGEMENTS

I am grateful to the editors of the following journals and anthologies in which versions of some of the poems and the prefatory essay in this volume have appeared or been recognized with distinction.

Hanging Loose: "37 Bennett Street," "Examples," and "English Lesson Plan: Present Perfect."

Red Brick Review: "Drift" and "Practicum."

City River of Voices, anthology (Denise Bergman, editor), West End Press: "Practicum" and "Lunch in Chinatown."

Voices of the City, an anthology (Robert Hershon and Marie Carter, editors): Rutgers University Center for Ethnicity, Culture and Modern Experience and Hanging Loose Press: "Drift" and "Examples."

36 New York Poets, poetry anthology, in Japanese translation (David Walton Wright and Takomi Eda, editors/translators), Shinchosha Publishing: "Drift."

UrbanArts/Boston Contemporary Authors Prize, engraved granite monolith, a permanent public art installation: "Drift."

Leuvre Litteraire: "Fashion Sense."

blog:ellensteinbaum.com, Reading and Writing and the Occasional Recipe: "Where the poem comes from: Mary Bonina."

The Teacher's Voice: A Journal for Poets and Writers in Education: *Lunch in Chinatown*, Finalist, national chapbook competition.

And... Thank You from the Author:

First and foremost, gratitude to my students who gave me these poems and the experience of so much joy being with them; the learning was mutual. I am especially grateful to Pui Ying Wong and Patrick Sylvain for reading the manuscript and commenting so generously; your own work inspires me. To those havens of peace and quiet and collegiality promoting the creation of new work: Vermont Studio Center, and especially the Virginia Center for the Creative Arts, and the Writers Room of Boston for supporting my work for years with residency fellowships and studio space. To Jean Flanagan and Arlington Center for the Arts for inviting me to read early versions of these poems way back when. To Denny Bergman, who was the first to publish any of these poems. To Ellen Steinbaum for her interest in my work. To the Cambridge Public Library for the freedom I had to create the Cambridge Public Library Literacy Project and direct it, offering affiliation, space and some financial support. To Gloria Mindock for seeing the enduring value of these poems and her work to bring them into the world with this publication.

And to my husband, poet Mark Pawlak for his love, encouragement, and support.

ABOUT THE AUTHOR

A fellow of the Virginia Center for the Creative Arts, Mary Bonina was finalist for the Goldfarb Fellowship and awarded several residencies, including one at the VCCA retreat, Moulin a Nef, in Auvillar, France. Previous publications include *My Father's Eyes: A Memoir* and two poetry collections—*Living Proof* and *Clear Eye Tea*, all from Červená Barva Press. Her poems and essays have appeared in *The Lowell Review, Hanging Loose, Poets and Writers, Salamander, Mom Egg, Ovunque Siamo, Adelaide,* and many other journals, and her work has been included in several anthologies, including *Entering The Real World, VCCA Poets on Mt. San Angelo* from Wavertree Press. Her completed novel, *My Way Home*, is on submission to publishers. Her poem "Drift" won *Boston Contemporary Authors/Urban Arts* prize and is carved in a granite monolith, a permanent public art installation in the City. Bonina has collaborated with composers of arts songs and new music, a sculptor, and her work has been translated into Japanese. She received a full fellowship from the Vermont Studio Center. A voiceover artist, she has recorded fiction, non-fiction, and poetry for blind readers. She offers classes, workshops, conference presentation, and individual coaching for writers. Bonina has been a long-time member of the Writers Room of Boston, where she served on the Board for more than a decade. She earned her M.F.A. in Fiction Writing from the Program for Writers at Warren Wilson College. She lives in Cambridge, Massachusetts. Her website is www.marybonina.com

Printed in the USA
CPSIA information can be obtained
at www.ICGtesting.com
LVHW050414300524
781140LV00001B/95